# DRONES AND ENTERTAINMENT

## LAURA LA BELLA

**ROSEN**
PUBLISHING

New York

Published in 2017 by The Rosen Publishing Group
29 East 21st Street, New York, NY 10010

Copyright 2017 by The Rosen Publishing Group, Inc.

First Edition

**Library of Congress Cataloging-in-Publication Data**

Names: La Bella, Laura, author.
Title: Drones and entertainment / Laura La Bella.
Description: First edition. | New York : Rosen Publishing, 2017. | Series:
Inside the world of drones | Includes bibliographical references and index.
Identifiers: LCCN 2016030848 | ISBN 9781508173397 (library bound)
Subjects: LCSH: Drone aircraft—United States—Juvenile literature. |
Aeronautics, Commercial—United States—Juvenile literature. |
Aeronautics, Commercial—Law and legislation—Juvenile literature. | News
agencies—Technological innovations—Juvenile literature. | Motion
pictures—Production and direction—Technological innovations—Juvenile
literature. | Technological innovations—Juvenile literature.
Classification: LCC UG1242.D7 L33 2017 | DDC 629.13—dc23
LC record available at https://lccn.loc.gov/2016030848


*Manufactured in China*

# CONTENTS

# INTRODUCTION

When we think of drones, we might imagine them used for surveillance and reconnaissance missions against military targets. But this is only one use of drones. Many more are emerging as drones become part of everyday life. These high-tech "eyes in the sky" are becoming more popular for a range of exciting nonmilitary civilian uses.

A new study by the Teal Group, a team of analysts covering the aerospace and defense industries, has estimated that by 2022, spending on drones will reach $89 billion. The vast majority of purchasers will be civilian, with private companies, media corporations, and individuals making wide use of drones for a range of activities.

Jason Lam, a professional photographer, is the owner of a personal drone store in San Francisco, California. He is already starting to cash in on the civilian drone trend. Lam's AeriCam sells drones to professional photographers and videographers who want to be able to capture images they can't with traditional cameras and camera equipment. In fact, drones are being used widely for a range of photography, media, art, and entertainment purposes. In the opening minutes of the feature film *Spring*, directors Justin Benson and Aaron Moorhead used a drone to film sweeping overhead shots of Italy. The 2015 US Open golf championship featured aerial footage courtesy of a drone. Real estate agents, who normally use a standard digital camera

DRONES LIKE THIS HEXACOPTER—NAMED FOR THE SIX MOTORS THAT ALLOW IT TO MOVE—WILL BECOME INCREASINGLY COMMON IN MEDIA, ENTERTAINMENT, AND OTHER CIVILIAN APPLICATIONS IN THE COMING YEARS.

to take photographs of a property can now use a drone to show encompassing aerial views of a property's land, neighborhood, and even the surrounding area. The BBC (British Broadcasting Company) was allowed to fly a drone along the tunnels of Crossrail, a large building project in London, England, that will interconnect trains and rail lines. The BBC featured the footage on a news report detailing the progress of the project. The uses of drones for photography, media, and entertainment are endless.

However, drone use is not without its limitations, nor is it free of controversy. The Federal Aviation Administration (FAA) has prohibited the widespread commercial use of drones, even though the demand for drones is high and their development by aerospace companies is rapid. To respond to this demand, the US Congress has asked the FAA to develop rules for drone use by any nonmilitary entities, which include private companies, media corporations, and individuals, such as photographers and filmmakers. The FAA has proposed some rules, but the agency is struggling to figure out how to keep up with and regulate an industry that is both very young and very dynamic in its ability to implement the newest in technologies.

Let us take a look now at some of the multifaceted uses of drones when it comes to media and entertainment. The future photographers, journalists, filmmakers, and many others in their respective fields are now entering a world where drone use will not be merely a curiosity, but an integral part of many creative fields.

# CHAPTER 1

# DRONES IN NEWS GATHERING

I n early 2012, Matt Waite, a professor in the College of Journalism and Mass Communications at the University of Nebraska-Lincoln, won a $50,000 grant from the Knight Foundation to launch a drone journalism program. Waite, a former journalist, established the Drone Journalism Lab to explore different ways drones could be used for reporting and gathering data.

Waite and a small team of students built and flew drones. Within a few months they were reporting on the local Nebraska landscape, which at the time was experiencing a severe drought. Soon after a letter arrived in the mail. It was a cease-and-desist order from the Federal Aviation Administration. The FAA, which regulates our national airspace, noticed Waite's activities and asked him and his

A DRONE HOVERS IN THE MIDDLE OF THE ROOM AT NEW YORK UNIVERSITY'S INTERACTIVE TELECOMMUNICATIONS PROGRAM (ITP) IN MAY 2014, IN NEW YORK, NEW YORK.

team to stop. The FAA has regulations in place to monitor the use of drones and, for safety reasons, to keep them from interfering with airspace that is used by commercial airlines and other aircraft. Understanding the origin of drones, their nature, and how they fly is crucial to understanding why the FAA must regulate their use.

## WHAT ARE DRONES?

A drone is any type of unmanned aircraft. They can be referred to as UAVs (unmanned aerial vehicles) or RPASs (remotely piloted aerial systems). Drones come in a range of sizes. They can be as small as a remote-controlled airplane or as large as a spy plane.

Drones differ in significant ways from remote-controlled airplanes, perhaps the machines most similar to drones. A remote-controlled airplane needs an operator engaged in every part of the flying process. It cannot do anything without the operator instructing it to via a remote control. Drones, however, are autonomous aircraft. With on-board computers programmed to carry out specific flight paths and tasks, such as surveillance or image gathering, a drone can fly where it is programmed to go. Drones can hover, fly, stay in a specific position in the sky, or navigate their surroundings without crew involvement.

Another key difference between a drone and a remote-controlled airplane is the involvement of the FAA. Hobbyists can fly model airplanes without any restrictions or oversight from the FAA. This is not the case with drones. It is illegal to fly a drone without special permission from the FAA. Once permission is granted, operators must follow a set of rules, which include flying below 400 feet (121 meters) and keeping the drone in the line of sight of its operator at all times. Drones also may not be used for any commercial reason unless the operator has received permission from the FAA. The agency can issue a "certificate of authorization" to public entities such as NASA, the National Oceanic and Atmospheric Administration, other federal agencies, police departments, or universities that want to use drones for special purposes.

## A TOOL FOR WAR

The September 11, 2001, terrorist attacks changed the way the US military and intelligence services used drones. With the US invasion of Afghanistan in response to 9/11, and its later invasion of Iraq, drones became a huge component of the United States' surveillance and attack capabilities.

Some drones are used for surveillance and reconnaissance, others are armed with missiles for targeted strikes. Drones can now be outfitted with still and video cameras, image intensifiers, ammunition, and various high-tech instruments that can process data in real time. Many drones deployed in the Middle East and Asia are even controlled by real-time operators on military bases in the American West.

# DIFFERENT TYPES OF DRONES

Depending on how you are planning to use a drone—whether it's for news gathering, at a sporting event, or to capture nature or wildlife in its natural habitats—a range of sizes and capabilities exist to help photographers or news reporters accomplish their goals. There is no classification system for drones like there is for vehicles (e.g., economy car, compact car, sports car) so drones are grouped by size, with smaller drones having fewer capabilities than larger ones.

*Very small drones*: Also called microdrones or nano-drones, very small drones can be as small as an insect or small bird. They are no larger than 19 inches (50 centimeters) long. Their small size makes them hard to notice, making them perfect for spying and gathering intelligence.

*Small drones*: Measuring between 19 and 78 inches (50 cm and 2 m), small drones do not take off and land autonomously. Instead, operators must throw them into the air for take off and aid in their landing. Small drones are often used for news gathering, photography, and sports coverage. They have a longer battery life than very small drones—up to 30 minutes—but are still small enough to remain unobtrusive.

*Medium drones*: More significant in weight and size—up to 440 pounds (199 kilograms) and with wingspans of 5 to 10 feet (1.5 to 3 m)—medium drones mirror small aircraft and are too large to be carried by a person.

*Large drones*: Used primarily by the military in combat situations, large drones can be the size of aircraft. They take off and land without assistance and are often armed with ammunition or missiles.

UNITED STATES MARINE SERGEANT NICHOLAS BENDER LAUNCHES A RAVEN SURVEILLANCE DRONE BY HAND NEAR BAQWA, IN SOUTHWEST AFGHANISTAN, ITS MISSION TO GATHER VALUABLE INTELLIGENCE ON THE TALIBAN.

# DRONES AND NEWS GATHERING

Even though revised FAA regulations are not yet complete, drones have still been used widely by journalists and news agencies. Under the current rules, journalists seeking an exemption from the FAA's restrictions must have a pilot's license before the FAA will grant their request. The FAA wants drone operators to understand how US aviation works and why drones are a potential hazard to commercial airliners and other aircraft flying in

US airspace. The certification program to obtain a pilot's license covers this in training.

The FAA has granted more than 3,000 exceptions to their rules, mostly to news organizations employing helicopter pilots and to those who have obtained pilot's licenses. Among the news agencies flying drones are CNN and broadcasters in the Cox Media Group, which include WSB in Atlanta, WFXT in Boston, and WFTV in Orlando. These stations have all begun using drones to report on news stories, weather conditions, breaking news, and more.

News agencies want to use drones for a wide range of reasons; most important, drones can access situations that

A JOURNALIST COVERING THE MURDER TRIAL OF OLYMPIC SPRINTER OSCAR PISTORIUS IN PRETORIA, SOUTH AFRICA, OPERATES A DRONE OUTSIDE THE COURTHOUSE TO OBTAIN BETTER FOOTAGE.

# DRONE JOURNALIST CODE OF ETHICS

The Society of Professional Journalists has four principles to its code of ethics for Journalists:

1. Seek truth and report it.
2. Minimize harm.
3. Act independently
4. Be accountable and transparent.

These rules encourage integrity in reporting. Similarly, the Professional Society of Drone Journalists has a code of ethics that offers an additional layer of consideration journalists should have when a drone is involved in the act of news gathering.

*Newsworthiness*: The investigation and reporting of a story should be significant enough to warrant the use of a drone. Drones should not be used if the information can be gathered in another way.

*Safety*: Drone operators should be trained in the operation of a drone and the equipment should be maintained properly for a safe and controlled flight. Drones should not be flown in questionable weather conditions or if the drone presents a hazard to the public.

*Sanctity of law and public spaces*: A drone journalist must follow airspace rules and regulations at all times and avoid being disruptive to the general public.

*Privacy*: Drone journalists should avoid invading the privacy of nonpublic figures and record only photographs or audio of events that occur in public spaces. Any images of individuals that are in the scope of the journalists' investigation should be censored or blocked to maintain privacy whenever possible.

*Traditional journalism ethics*: Drone journalists should follow the traditional journalism code of ethics in all of their drone reporting.

are too risky for a reporter or videographer. As much as journalists like to be on the front line of stories, there are some places they just can't go, whether it's for safety or other reasons. Drones can gather video from areas of conflict where it is too dangerous for a reporter or videographer to be on the ground. They can offer a bird's-eye view of forest fires or other natural disasters in areas too dangerous or impossible to traverse. Drones also can take aerial shots of crowds at events. This can keep reporters and videographers safe. They can also reach areas where reporters cannot gain access, such as floods, wildfires, and other remote areas. Drone use also offers an affordable alternative to expensive helicopters, like those used by new stations and major broadcasters.

# THE FIRST AMENDMENT VERSUS THE FAA

Most members of the media favor relaxing the rules on using drones for news gathering and reporting. But current FAA regulations make this difficult. The FAA is moving toward formulating final regulations that will govern the use of drones in public airspace—regulations that likely will decide if drones can even be used in news gathering and how drones can be used effectively by the media. In a memo released to news agencies in May 2015, the FAA said that a news agency can use a drone if the FAA has provided authorization. If an agency does not have permission, then the agency can purchase images taken by a recreational or hobby drone user that is not affiliated with a news agency. But this suggestion is limited to news agencies. Recreational drone operators must stay 500 feet (152 m) away from people, vehicles, and structures, and they must ensure safety in the event the drone crashes. Media agencies were unhappy with this suggested use of citizen journalism.

The media have also decided not to simply wait on a ruling by the FAA without their input. A coalition of media companies, including the *New York Times*, Associated Press, and *Washington Post*, drafted a legal brief for the FAA that takes the position that the First Amendment, which includes freedom of the press, prevents the FAA from blocking news reporting in any way, which in this modern age, could easily include the use of drones to investigate and report on newsworthy stories.

# CHAPTER 2

# IN TELEVISION AND FILM PRODUCTION

I n the 2012 blockbuster film *Skyfall*, secret agent James Bond pursues a terrorist over the rooftops of Istanbul's famous bazaar in an explosive motorbike chase. *Expendables 3* featured a dramatic rescue attempt with a helicopter exchanging gunfire with prison guards aboard a speeding train. Filming every exciting twist and turn in these productions was a drone.

Drones have become popular tools for directors and cinematographers, who are using the unmanned aircrafts to film stunning vistas, exciting aerial shots of action, and overhead crowd shots in a wide range of film media. Drone technology is ushering in a new era of television and film-making, as well as advertising production.

AN ENGINEER FOR THE FRENCH MULTIMEDIA FIRM TECHNICOLOR S.A. DEMONSTRATES HOW A DRONE IS USED TO PRE-VISUALIZE CAMERA EFFECTS IN THE FILMMAKING PROCESS.

## MEDIA FAA EXEMPTIONS

The film and television industry is reaping the benefits of a set of exemptions by the FAA that granted six aerial photo and video production companies permission to use drones to film footage for movies, commercials, and TV shows. Filmmakers, directors, and cinematographers are happy with the exemption, because it allows for more creative filming options.

With drones, filmmakers can get more distinctive and inventive shots, because drones can go where helicopters and other manned aircraft cannot, such as dropping low into an alley, following an action sequence from above a crowd, filming breathtaking scenery in exotic, hard-to-reach locales, and even flying through doors and windows.

While drone use on movie and TV sets is not common-place—just 10 percent of all productions use drones—interest by filmmakers, directors, and cinematographers in using the devices to shoot complicated scenes or to provide a new perspective for the audience is growing. Even with the FAA's exemption, restrictions and limitations are still in place, and need to be honored by the production companies that received the exemptions. These restrictions include:

- Drones may only be used in restricted areas where filming will take place.
- Drones must be flown under 400 feet (121 m) and for no longer than 30 minutes at a time.
- Nighttime flights are currently prohibited.
- Under the current rules, reality television shows or other unscripted events do not qualify for drone permits.
- All drone operators are required to have up-to-date pilot's licenses, with three-person crews for all flights.
- Safety guidelines must be adhered to at all times. These include being at least 17 years of age and getting a certificate from the FAA to fly a drone. Operators can only fly one drone at a time, and drones must be available for inspection upon request by the FAA. Drones must be flown within sight of their operators at all times.

A DRONE CONTROLLED BY DIRECTOR CEDRIC KLAPISCH FOLLOWS AND FILMS POLE VAULTER RENAULD LAVIELLENIE IN FRANCE, AS PART OF A DOCUMENTARY ABOUT TRAINING FOR THE 2016 OLYMPICS.

## BENEFITS TO TV/FILM PRODUCTION

The advantages of using drones extend beyond just being able to get a unique or different type of shot for a film or television production. Drone use can be less expensive, more convenient, easier, and more reliable. Directors have more flexibility for exciting and one-of-a-kind shots, and they can help save a production significant amounts of money. Cost is just one of several benefits of using drones for film and television productions.

# FILM FESTIVALS FOR DRONE FOOTAGE

Every filmmaker wants to show off his or her work. A film festival is an organized, extended presentation of films that takes place over a set number of days. Film festivals highlight different and unique ways filmmakers tell their stories. Drone film festivals honor the talent of filmmakers who choose to use a drone for filming. Festivals may include categories for genres, such as narrative, technical, landscape/architecture, amateur, long form, short feature, sports film, documentary, and more.

Each festival has its own submission guidelines, which can include limits on length of the film and what percentage of the film must be shot via drone.

To date there are more than 25 film festivals around the world that celebrate and feature drone filmmaking. These festivals include Blue2Blue in Australia, Drone Experience Festival in France, Rise of the Drones Film Festival in the United Kingdom, Peugeot Drone Film Festival in Germany, DroneUp International Film Festival in Bulgaria, as well as several in the United States, such as the New York City Drone Film Festival in New York, Bridger Cup Drone Film Festival in Missouri, and F3 Expo in Atlanta, Georgia.

*Less expensive:* A camera and mount currently used on helicopters can cost up to one million dollars depending on the shoot. By contrast, a camera-mounted drone can shoot similar footage with possible better angles or more inventive shots, and can cost a few thousand dollars.

*Green technology:* Drones are a greener option than helicopters. "Green" refers to being environmentally friendly or being conscious of how the use of technology can negatively impact our environment and implementing measures to minimize these impacts. The average helicopter can consume more than 35 gallons (132 l) of fuel per hour of flight. Drones are powered by rechargeable batteries and emit no exhaust emissions into the air.

*Convenient:* Because of the smaller size of a drone, a location shoot does not have to worry about where a helicopter can land and be stored if it will be used over several days, or where it will refuel, especially if the location is remote, such as a desert.

*Easy, fast set-up:* Drones can be ready to fly within 10 minutes and can be producing images as soon as they are in position in the air.

*More maneuverable:* Drones can operate indoors, outdoors, at any hour of the day (nighttime shoots are currently prohibited), in any location, and in light-to-moderate weather conditions.

*Less intrusive:* Drones are quicker than helicopters. They also have no downdraft, which is the wind produced by the blades of a helicopter. These differences mean that dialogue and other sounds can be recorded even if a drone is hovering above.

*Safer:* Drones are a safer option than helicopters, which present a riskier filming experience for a camera crew.

THIS DRONE AT THE COMMERCIAL UAV SHOW IN LONDON DURING OCTOBER 2014 IS A UAV FROM FLAIRICS GMBH AND CO., AUGMENTED BY A SONY DIGITAL CAMERA. LATE 2014 SAW EASING OF RESTRICTIONS ON DRONE FILMMAKING.

Another related and favorable feature of drones is their ability to get the same desired shots without time-consuming, expensive, and potentially disruptive filming set-ups. A ground-based shot may require dozens of people working long hours. In areas that are sensitive—such as places of natural beauty—or places where people live, work, or commute, filming might be otherwise banned. Nonintrusive drone filmmaking may be palatable for governments, residents, and others who must give media producers permits and permissions.

# A CAREER AS AN AERIAL DRONE PHOTOGRAPHER

Drone photography is an exciting subfield of photography that is growing in popularity. An aerial drone photographer is a professional photographer who captures images from the air. Traditionally, aerial photographers have used any type of flying or floating device, from kites and hot air balloons to helicopters and hang gliders. But an aerial drone photographer uses an unmanned aircraft to capture the images they want. To become an aerial drone photographer, you'll need a mix of education, including photography skills, as well as a pilot's license and general knowledge of drone technology.

*Job description*—An aerial drone photographer is tasked with obtaining images from the air using a drone. Aerial photographs are needed for a wide variety of uses, including land surveying, mapmaking, artistic purposes, and more.

*Educational requirements*—Any pro aerial drone photographer needs a solid foundation in photography. A degree in photography is strongly encouraged. Photography degrees cover topics such as image making, photographic technologies, digital photography, photographic techniques, architectural photography, production photography, shooting on location, lighting, and more. Students in high school can begin to prepare themselves for a career in photography by taking introductory photography courses as well as art classes. If you intend to operate your own business as an aerial drone photographer, basic business courses will be essential. These can help you gain knowledge of accounting practices, managerial skills, business development, and marketing.

*Pilot's license*—An aerial drone photographer is required by the FAA to have a pilot's license. A pilot's license provides an understanding of the US air system as well as rules, regulations, and safety considerations an aerial drone photographer will need to be aware of as they fly their aircraft. Obtaining a pilot's license includes training, course work, and flight experience.

*Drone aircraft knowledge*—Understanding how to fly and maintain your drone is a necessary part of your job as an aerial drone photographer. You may need to repair your drone, know how to recharge its battery, and perform basic maintenance.

## A LEVEL PLAYING FIELD FOR MEDIA PRODUCERS

Drones have the potential to level the playing field between big studios and independent filmmakers and producers, and between professional photographers and those starting out. Big production studios often have multimillion dollar budgets for films, which enable a director or producer to have the money for a helicopter and other more expensive filming equipment.

Independent movie studios and individual filmmakers often have restrictive budgets which dictate what a director can and cannot afford to do on a production. For independents, the affordability of purchasing and using a drone makes it easier for independent filmmakers and individual photographers with tighter budgets to produce impressive pieces of work that are the same scale and professional level as big studios. The use of drones may be as freeing and empowering for young and beginning filmmakers on limited budgets as the digital film camera revolution has been in the last two decades. Their mobility and flexibility will also surely help them greatly expand the creative horizons of cinematography.

# CHAPTER 3

# DRONES IN PHOTOGRAPHY

Not long ago, there was a period of time when an individual could fly a drone virtually anywhere in the world. It was between the periods when drones were introduced as nonmilitary devices and the inception of regulations and laws created to control and monitor their use.

Amos Chapple, a New Zealand travel photographer, took advantage of this brief lapse in regulation. Not long ago, Chapple spent two years visiting 16 different countries to capture images of some of the world's most iconic sites. Using a drone, Chapple was able to photograph dramatic images of India's Taj Mahal; the star fort at Bourtange, Netherlands; the Kauri Cliffs golf course in New Zealand; Saint Isaac's Cathedral in St. Petersburg, Russia; the Sacré-Cœur cathedral in

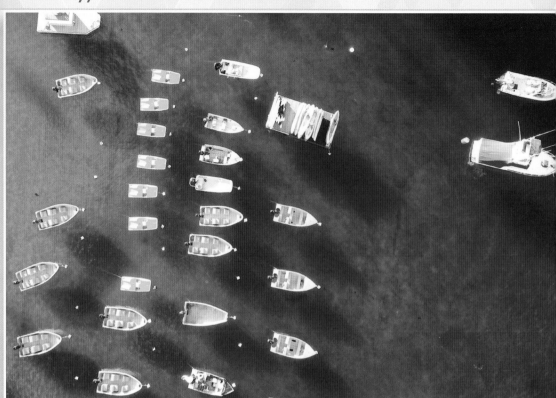

THIS AERIAL SHOT TAKEN FROM ABOVE OF BOATS DOCKED NEAR CATALINA ISLAND, OFF THE SOUTHERN CALIFORNIA COAST, IS AN EXAMPLE OF ONE OF THE MANY PHOTOGRAPHIC POSSIBILITIES THAT DRONES OPEN UP.

Paris, France; Sagrat Cor Church in Barcelona, Spain; and the Vittoria Light on the Gulf of Trieste in Italy. Because he used a drone, most of his images are the only ones of their kind.

Photographers of all kinds are now using drones to capture images in new ways. Drones enable them to view subjects from higher in the air, at better angles, and achieve different perspectives and more interesting shots.

# DRONES AND THE WORLD OF ART

In addition to influencing the world of photography, drones are being used by artists to create interactive exhibitions and live performances to bring people closer to art.

Cirque du Soleil's *Sparked* is a live interactive performance between humans and drones, with 10 quadcopter drones carrying out the kind of complex synchronized dance maneuvers audiences see from the circus's human acrobats. The drones are designed to look like lampshades of various colors and sizes. They dance and interact along with human performers.

From August through September 2015, *First Person View* was a month-long show at the Knockdown Center in Maspeth, New York, an arts space on the border of Brooklyn and Queens. The installation invited people to physically pilot drones up to, around, and through a series of nine artworks. The installation incorporated the drone's point of view as a new way of looking at and appreciating art. Visitors were encouraged to bring their own drones to use in the exhibit.

Drone footage is also being used more commonly in artworks, media installations, museum exhibitions, and more.

## TRAVEL PHOTOGRAPHY

Chapple is a travel photographer and drones are having an impact on how he and others in his field are capturing

THIS DRONE SHOT OF A GEOTHERMAL PLANT IN ICELAND DEMONSTRATES ANOTHER PERSPECTIVE THAT CAN BE ACHIEVED WITHOUT EXPENSIVE MANNED AERIAL PHOTOGRAPHY.

images of the world's most amazing places and sites. Drones, with their ability to hover over the action, can capture a kayaker paddling toward a stunning waterfall, the immense vistas of a desert or mountain range, life in the hidden world of Earth's oceans, and more. Before drones became an affordable alternative, most of these images required utilizing helicopters and hot air balloons. Now, professional photographers, recreational hobbyists, and entrepreneurs have an opportunity to access locations they never could to capture more creative images of the world.

## REAL ESTATE PHOTOGRAPHY

A growing demand for drone photography is in the real estate sector. Real estate agents sell and rent properties for a living, often posting pictures of homes, offices, or empty lots. Pictures show customers what the bedrooms, kitchen, dining room, and other living spaces look like.

For large commercial properties, such as manufacturing facilities or large tracts of rural land, photographing them from the ground doesn't always capture their size and scope. A drone, however, can provide aerial photography and video of commercial properties, giving buyers a better sense of what the listing has to offer and if it's worth visiting in person.

Internationally, drones are used regularly to capture images of real estate listings. The National Association of Realtors (NAR) has been pushing the FAA to allow real estate agents to use drones. In support of their efforts, the NAR has created a list of frequently asked questions on their website to address the use of drones and best practices for their agents to follow when and if drones are approved for this use.

# PHOTOGRAPHING THE NATURAL WORLD

Nature photography encompasses all the types of images that show the beauty and awe-inspiring scenery of the natural world. Nature photography is divided into two categories: nature and wildlife. "Nature" refers to images of things like landscapes, geologic formations, and weather phenomena. "Wildlife" refers to animals in both their natural habitats as well as in controlled environments, such as zoos and aquariums. Normally, people are not featured in these images, the focus instead being on the natural subject. These images also have an emphasis on the aesthetic, artistic, or visual value of the photo.

Montingegnoli Castle is shown in this drone photo. Travel photographers and tourism promoters can put drones to good use in depicting and promoting historical sites.

Many nature photographers (or their sponsors, like publications or nonprofits) hire a small airplane or helicopter to take them up into the sky to shoot aerial images of nature and landscapes. It's an expensive and also limiting endeavor. Aircraft usually fly about 1,000 feet (304 m) above the ground and a photographer must use a wide-angle or telephoto lens to shoot. The height can impact the detail the photographer is attempting to get in his or her shot. Drones, however, fly at much lower elevations, usually under 400 feet (121 m), which means a photographer can hone in on details in a rock formation, show more variations in the color of a sunset, or shoot a landscape at a more intimate angle.

Nature photographers who specialize in wildlife photography use drones as a way to be less intrusive to the habitats and behaviors of their animal subjects. Michael Nichols, an award-winning photographer, spent two years living with a pride of lions on the Serengeti Plain in Tanzania. He used the time to document the daily lives of the lion pride and to photograph them like no one has been able to before. To accomplish this he used a drone.

Photographing the lions close-up and on the ground posed a risk to Nichols and his crew. It also posed a risk to the lion pride as well. Because lions sleep all day and are up hunting most of the night, Nichols and his team worked through the night on several occasions. And, because the drones are quiet and pose little intrusion to the animals, Nichols was able to capture images without disturbing the lions' regular

DRONES PROVIDE NON-INTRUSIVE AND UNIQUE ANGLES FOR PHOTOGRAPHERS, CONSERVATIONISTS, SCIENTISTS, AND OTHERS STUDYING ANIMALS, SUCH AS THESE SEA LIONS OFF THE COAST OF SOUTHEAST ALASKA.

habits and routines. Nichol's photos were used in an August 2013 issue of *National Geographic* magazine.

Drones have played a significant role in wildlife photography and wildlife preservation. A team of filmmakers used a drone to film the Serengeti for a TV documentary in Japan. Researchers in Kenya are beginning to use drones to monitor areas where rhino poaching has occurred. In addition to taking photographs, researchers and conservationists are able to use drones to better keep track of animals, document changes in their numbers, and monitor dangers presented by humans, such as poaching and hunting.

# INFRARED PHOTOGRAPHY

Just beyond the light spectrum that the human eye can detect is infrared light, a type of light we cannot see without the aid of a special lens. All types of objects reflect infrared light in different ways. Their colors, textures, elements of nature, such as leaves and plants, human skin, and the sky, show differently in infrared light. Through the use of special films or sensors, which have infrared light sensitivity, photographers are able to capture images in complete darkness or photograph a subject that is reflecting infrared light. In both cases, the images will look very different from images shot using light from the visible part of the spectrum. Drones can be equipped with infrared cameras and, with their ability to access all types of terrain and locations,

# A NEW APP FOR DRONE OPERATORS

Google Maps is one of the most widely used mapping applications used for driving. Google is hoping Hivemapper will do the same for drone operators. Drivers have a full view of their surroundings by looking out their front windshield and their passenger and rear windows.

With a drone, an operator can only see in one direction at a time. Hivemapper is attempting to change that by mapping out the airspace around bridges, antennas, buildings, and other natural and man-made structures. Hivemapper, which can be downloaded for both Android and Apple devices, will be able to tell a drone operator how many feet you are from a building, if power lines or electrical wires are in the vicinity, and at what height your drone needs to be to clear a structure like a bridge or antenna.

Currently, the app is compatible with a limited number of drones. As of November 2015, the boundaries and heights of more than 20 million buildings and 15 million places of interest in the United States have been pinpointed for Hivemapper, with more being mapped every day. Thousands of no-fly zones, which are designated areas of airspace that aircraft of any kind are not permitted to fly over, are also on Hivemapper. No-fly zones include high-security locations, like the White House or the Pentagon, and locations where security is sensitive, such as military bases and nuclear power plants.

enable photographers to get infrared images they might not be able to capture any other way.

# BROUGHT TO LIFE AND UP CLOSE: CONCERTS AND EVENTS

Front row seats to a concert by a popular performer are usually never cheap. If you want a shot or video, your view from ground level might not be satisfactory. Now, the best vantage point to filming or photographing a concert or other live event is in the air above the crowds, with a drone.

Drones are taking to the skies above audiences to capture video and still photography of concerts and events. Drones are not limited to the angles a person is able to see by standing in the crowd or even sitting on someone else's shoulders. Drones can fly above crowds, weave close to the stage to get close-up shots, and even maneuver around, above, and behind performers to capture the action. Drones are also less intrusive and less disruptive to the audience and the performers themselves.

Of course, for most commercial events, bands and other performers (and venues) will likely hire their own official film making drone operator or team. There will still be restrictions to who can film where, depending on whether an event is free, who it is promoted or sanctioned by, and who you know. But fans stand to benefit even if they themselves are not filming it firsthand. Platforms like YouTube, official concert videos, and other places where such incredible new footage is purveyed make it a win-win situation for music and other enthusiasts.

# CHAPTER 4

# SPORTS AND DRONES

At more than 80 miles (129 km) per hour, Olympic skiers fly down the side of a mountain racing for glory. At the 2014 Sochi Winter Olympic Games, skiers had a companion following them on the slopes. Drones, armed with hi-tech photography and video equipment, zoomed along ski trails and down hill courses capturing every harrowing twist and turn of the icy slopes.

The Sochi Olympiad was the first Olympic Games to use drones. Dispatched to film skiing and snowboarding events, the drones were able to capture athletes in action. Their size, flexibility in their ability to maneuver around athletes, and quiet operation made them a valuable tool to broadcasters covering the games.

# CLOSER TO THE ACTION

Sports broadcasters are hoping that drones will help them take viewers closer to the action on the field, on the court, on the slopes, and wherever sporting events are taking place. The Sochi Olympics isn't the only event to have drones hovering overhead. The 2015 US Open gold championship used drones to offer viewers different angles and to provide more comprehensive action on the links.

Drones used for sporting events are equipped with high-definition cameras, real-time video downloads, and in some cases, the ability to record audio. They can deliver the high quality shots sports networks like ESPN, Fox Sports, and other sports broadcasting stations rely on. One of the biggest advantages of

AN OVERHEAD SHOT OF A SWIMMING COMPETITION NEAR REYKJAVIK, ICELAND, PROVIDES AN EXAMPLE OF HOW DRONES CAN ENHANCE SPORTS PHOTOGRAPHY.

using drones is their flexibility. Traditional sports coverage has several camera crews set up at various points around a sporting event. A director in a control room either at a broadcast station or onsite in a control booth or broadcast truck directs the production. As play changes on the field or court, for example, the director tells the production which camera shot to feature in the broadcast. Drones, however, are more proactive in their ability to capture the action. As play changes direction, so can a drone. Drones can also get closer to the action than fixed cameras. A drone can respond to the action on the field instead of a director telling a crew which camera shot is necessary.

DRONES CAN ALSO PROVIDE RICH, COLORFUL FOOTAGE AND IMAGES OF SPORTS VENUES AND OTHER EVENT SITES, BOTH UP CLOSE AND FROM A GREAT DISTANCE.

# ATHLETE TRAINING

Drones in sports are being used creatively, even beyond broadcasting sporting events. The coaching staff of the Division I football team at the University of California at Los Angeles (UCLA) uses drones to film practice footage of their football team running plays and completing passing drills. The footage is analyzed later by the team's coaching staff, who are looking at the foot placement of players, the spacing between the members of the offensive line, the hand placement of the center lineman who hands the ball to the quarterback, and the field positioning of wide receivers as they run a route to catch a pass. With closer video coverage of athletes in practice, small tweaks to game play can make big differences in athletic performance and outcomes. Coaches now have a way to capture close-up images to help them make these types of corrections.

NOTE THE DRONE HOVERING OVERHEAD WHILE THESE FOOTBALL PLAYERS FROM THE UNIVERSITY OF MIAMI TRAIN IN CORAL GABLES, FLORIDA.

# THE DOWNSIDE OF DRONES IN SPORTS BROADCASTING

Drones are not without their disadvantages when it comes to capturing athletic events. For all of their abilities, drones do have some limitations. In some ways, these may apply to recording other public events, like concerts, political rallies, and public meetings.

*Battery life:* For the smaller drones used in sports broadcasting, battery life is not long enough for the duration of an event. The National Football League, as well as some college football programs, regularly use cable-suspended cameras to get aerial shots during games. These cameras are suspended high above the action on the field and can operate the full length of the game. By contrast, many drones still only have a 20 to 30 minutes of battery life.

*Disrupting the fan experience:* As exciting as it is for fans to see a game from a new angle, drones can be disruptive to the fan experience. A drone hovering above a rolling golf course can be a jarring sight. Drones can also interfere with the sight lines of fans who paid money to attend an event to see the game being played.

*Potential for accidents:* The sporting experience itself could be compromised by the presence of a drone. Sports broadcasters are careful to never influence or disrupt play or cause harm to fans by broadcasting an event.

But accidents have happened with drones. A student flying a drone during pregame events at the University of

# START YOUR DRONES: FLYING COMPETITIONS

Drones are ready to go from broadcasting sports to becoming participants. Drone pilot and builder Erich Bitonio gathered along with a few dozen drone pilots at the sixth annual World Maker Faire 2015 DIY festival in Queens, New York, to announce the launch of Aerial Sports League, an organization that wants to create sporting competitions for drones and their operators. These events, which could range from racing, obstacle courses, combat piloting, and fixed-wing maneuvers, would test drone operators' skills and talents in manipulating the abilities of a drone.

The Aerial Sports League website lists events, and there is already a US National Drone Racing Championships competition. Drone racing leagues are popping up across the country, including the Drone Racing League in New York, where daring individuals interested in pushing the boundaries of drone technologies gather to build, test, fly, and compete with drones. It's not only techies who are interested in watching drones race and fight. ESPN is also on board, and other broadcasters are starting to notice. The sports network announced that it will cover a three-day drone racing event in New York in late 2016. Drone racing is not just an American trend. A drone racing event in Dubai, United Arab Emirates, offered over $1 million in prize money to winners.

DRONE OPERATORS, LIKE THIS ONE USING A UAW TO FILM A CRICKET GAME IN WELLINGTON, NEW ZEALAND, ARE EVER MORE COMMON DURING BOTH SPORTS PRACTICES AND COMPETITIONS.

Kentucky's first home football game of the season crashed the drone into the side of the press box at Commonwealth Stadium. During the final women's tennis match of the US Open, a New York City high school teacher flew a drone into Louis Armstrong Stadium, where it hovered above the heads of professional tennis players Flavia Pennetta and Monica Niculescu, who were playing against one another for the championship. The drone crashed in the stands. In a news conference after the match Pennetta said she though the drone was a bomb. The University of Kentucky now prohibits the use of drones on its campus, and the US Open has restricted their use in covering tennis matches.

# FAA RULINGS

The FAA has issued rules that prohibit drone use at certain sporting events. At all NFL, Major League Baseball, and Division I college football games, drones are prohibited from flying within three nautical miles of the event. This ban lasts from one hour before game time to one hour after. Drones are also prohibited at most NASCAR and INDY car races. In some cases, depending on the event, the regulation can be expanded in cases where public safety is a significant concern.

In January 2015, when the Superbowl was hosted at the University of Phoenix Stadium in Glendale, Arizona, the FAA issued an order establishing restricted flight zones around the event. While a 10-mile (16 km) ring banned everything but law enforcement and government aircraft, and a 30-mile (48 km) outer ring heavily restricted all other flights, drones and other unmanned craft were entirely banned within the outer ring.

# CHAPTER 5

# THE LEGAL HORIZON

Drones can go anywhere, but in some cases, that might present more of a problem than an opportunity. Pop star Miley Cyrus posted a video to her social media accounts showing a drone hovering over her backyard, attempting to take photographs of the singer in and around her private California home.

## AN ASSAULT ON PRIVACY

For all the positives that drones offer, whether it's in the fields of entertainment, photography, sports, law enforcement, or warfare, there is always the risk that these eyes in the sky will capture images of things they shouldn't. Privacy is among the most controversial topics when the conversation turns to drones and their use. The legal environment has been slow to react to this rapidly developing technology, and its ever more rapid rollout.

When it comes to celebrities, athletes, and politicians, some states have been proactive in passing laws to protect the privacy of these public figures. The state of California, especially the film capital of the United States in Los Angeles, is home to many prying paparazzi. These professional photographers follow celebrities, entertainers, athletes, and politicians to photograph them and sell the images for profit.

Paparazzi aren't your average photographers, they are often considered bounty hunters, since their work can produce significant paychecks for an image of a high profile individual, a new celebrity baby, or a newly married celebrity couple. Because of this, paparazzi often bend the law to pursue their livelihood. Some even engage in car chases, trespass onto private property, and otherwise break the law in order to get a lucrative series of photos.

For paparazzi, the appeal of using a drone is obvious: Why should a photographer hide in a tree or in the bushes with a telephoto lens to catch a celebrity sunbathing in the privacy of their backyard when he or she can launch a drone and let the device do the work for them?

Luckily for public figures, California has passed a law that prohibits the use of a drone in the airspace above a person's private property to capture any images or video of that person engaged in private, personal, or family activities. Paparazzi can no longer use drones to invade the privacy of a public person on private property.

PROTESTERS BELONGING TO A GROUP CALLED STOP LAPD SPYING COALITION PROTEST IN LOS ANGELES, CALIFORNIA, IN FRONT OF CITY HALL, AGAINST THE POTENTIAL USE OF DRONES TO VIOLATE CITIZENS' RIGHTS.

# PRIVACY AND THE FOURTH AMENDMENT

The Fourth Amendment rights of all people in America theoretically ensure a certain degree of privacy. Drones, with their ability to record audio as well as take video and still photography, make it easier to eavesdrop on individuals with increasing ease and in many cases, in secret. The Fourth Amendment protects individuals from electronic surveillance and from illegal search and seizure, which means law enforcement agencies cannot search your home, person, or personal effects unless sufficient evidence strongly indicates wrongdoing. Even with sufficient evidence, a search warrant must be issued by a judge before a search can begin.

Drones have the ability to conduct surveillance, which is the close observation of people or activities, and to record personal, private conversations. This presents the opportunity for a drone and its operator to capture audio or images that could be intrusive to a person's privacy or, if wrongdoing has occurred, provide evidence of a crime. To date, there have not been any court cases that have been brought against a drone operator for eavesdropping on an individual, but the potential is strong that as more and more people use drones, the risk for these situations to emerge is great.

# A THAW ON DRONE RESTRICTIONS?

The US Congress passed a new law, called the FAA Reauthorization Act, in February 2012 that opens national airspace to drones for commercial, scientific, and law enforcement use. US President Barack Obama, known for aggressive use of military drone warfare overseas, signed the bill into law. The law requires the FAA to establish regulations for drone use by 2015. It also created a system for licensing drones, which requires all drone operators to register their drones every two years with the FAA. With registration, each drone is assigned a number that enables authorities to track down a drone's owner if the drone violates FAA regulations, such as flying too close to an airport, flying into commercial airspace used by airplanes, colliding with another aircraft, or entering no-fly zones.

In 2015, the Drone Aircraft Privacy and Transparency Act was passed to address concerns about drone aircraft and the intentions of their operators. The act requires private drone operators to submit a data collection statement to the FAA prior to receiving a drone operating license. The act requires operators to list their name, where the drone will be operated, the type of data the drone will collect, how

U.S. SENATOR PAT LEAHY OF VERMONT (*LEFT*, FLANKED BY SENATOR AL FRANKEN) HOLDS UP A DRAGANFLYER X6 DRONE AT A SENATE JUDICIARY COMMITTEE MEETING ABOUT LAW ENFORCEMENT AND PRIVACY IN MARCH 2013.

# THE CURRENT STATE OF DRONE LAWS

While the FAA debates how to regulate drones in our national airspace, some states are not waiting for federal guidelines to be drafted before creating local laws restricting drone use.

Arizona has passed a law that prohibits certain uses of drones, including any use of a drone that interferes with first responders and operating a drone near, or taking images of, critical state infrastructure such as bridges, nuclear power plants, or energy systems.

A MODEL DRONE LOOMS ABOVE AN OCTOBER 2013 PROTEST AGAINST FEDERAL GOVERNMENT SURVEILLANCE IN WASHINGTON, D.C. MANY MEMBERS OF THE PUBLIC ARE SKEPTICAL OF DRONES DUE TO GOVERNMENT ABUSES.

Virginia requires all law enforcement agencies to obtain a warrant before using a drone for any purpose. The only exceptions are in emergency situations or training exercises designed to improve responses to emergency situations.

Indiana prohibits the use of drones to scout game during hunting season.

Kansas expanded the state's definition of harassment in the Protection from Stalking Act to include the use of drones to spy on, harass, or otherwise intimidate.

Wisconsin prohibits the use of a drone in hunting, fishing, or trapping, and the state prohibits flying a drone over a correctional facility.

the data will be used, and whether the information will be sold to a third party. The act was passed to help ensure that drone operators' intentions are honorable and pose no risk to the privacy rights of individual citizens.

Some individual states have taken the law into their own hands and have passed state-level laws addressing drone use. According to the Association for Unmanned Vehicle Systems International, at least six states—Florida, Minnesota, Nevada, North Dakota, Oregon, and Virginia—have passed legislation restricting the commercial use of drones. Another eight have restrictive legislation pending.

# DRONE JOURNALISM AND THE FIRST AMENDMENT

The field of journalism, in particular the freedom of the press, is theoretically protected by our rights under the First Amendment. Legal experts are arguing that drone use in journalism may violate journalists' First Amendment rights. Under existing laws, photographing and filming (though not necessarily audio recording) events that are newsworthy or are of the public interest, and that occur in public places, falls under the First Amendment right of freedom of expression. That means that camera-equipped drones used in news gathering are protected by the First Amendment, even though the FAA is preparing regulations that may infringe upon their use, and defends its actions as a necessary limit for the security and safety of the skies.

# GLOSSARY

**AERIAL** Of or pertaining to the air.

**AMATEUR** A person who engages in an activity as a hobbyist, and is not paid; for example, an amateur athlete.

**ANALYST** A person who conducts analysis of a topic or subject.

**AUTONOMOUS** The ability to act independently.

**CINEMATOGRAPHY** The art form of motion picture photography, which is key to how movies and television shows look.

**CITIZEN** A legally recognized subject or national of a nation or state, whether born into citizenship or naturalized.

**CIVILIAN** Describes a person or thing that is not part of or related to the military or law enforcement—for example, civilian drone use includes those used by private citizens or other private-sector entities, such as corporations, nonprofits, or government agencies.

**COMPLIANCE** Following rules or regulations put in place by an official body, such as a regulatory agency.

**DIVISION I** The highest class of college level sports.

**DOCUMENTARY** A film that purports to provide a factual accounting of a real-life event or phenomenon.

**EAVESDROP** To secretly listen in on a conversation.

**ELEVATION** The height of something above a certain level; for example, elevation above sea level.

**ETHICS** Principles that govern a person or group's behavior, especially when it comes to right or wrong.

**EXEMPTION** A legal pass that enables an organization to ignore certain rules or regulations.

**NARRATIVE** A story or account.

**NAUTICAL MILE** A measurement based on the circumference of the Earth and used for charting and navigation on water.

**PAPARAZZI** Independent photographers, often aggressive and sometimes perceived to be morally questionable, who take pictures of public figures such as celebrities, athletes, or politicians, in hopes of a big payout from those who will purchase their photos, like media companies.

**PROTOTYPE** A preliminary model of something that will be made or manufactured later.

**QUADCOPTER** A multi-rotor helicopter or drone that typically uses two clockwise and two counterclockwise fixed propellers.

**SANCTITY** The state of being holy or sacred.

**STATUTE** A written law that is passed by a legislative body or declared by an organization or group.

**SURVEILLANCE** Close observation of a person or place, often conducted secretly or unobtrusively.

**TELEPHOTO** A long-focus lens used to capture images of something far away.

# FOR MORE INFORMATION

Academy of Model Aeronautics
5161 E. Memorial Drive
Muncie, IN 47302
(800) 435-9262
Website: http://www.modelaircraft.org
With more than 175,000 members, the Academy of Model Aeronautics is the
world's largest model aviation association.

Airborne Law Enforcement Association
50 Carroll Creek Way, Suite 260
Frederick, MD 21701
(301) 631-2406
Website: http://alea.org
The Airborne Law Enforcement Association is a nonprofit educational
organization that supports and encourages the use of aircraft in public safety.
The organization offers educational seminars and training as well as general
information.

American Society of Cinematographers (ASC)
PO Box 2230
Los Angeles, CA 90028
(800) 448-0145
Website: http://www.theasc.com
The American Society of Cinematographers (ASC) is a professional association of
cinematographers who exchange ideas, discuss techniques, and promote film
making and films as an art form.

Association of Unmanned Vehicle Systems International (AUVSI)
2700 S. Quincy Street, Suite 400
Arlington, VA 22206
(703) 845 9671
Website: http://www.auvsi.org
AUVSI is the world's largest nonprofit organization devoted to advancing the drone,
unmanned systems, and robotics community.

Canadian Centre for Unmanned Vehicle Systems
#4, 49 Viscount Avenue SW
Medicine Hat, AB  T1A 5G4
Canada
(403) 488-7208
Website: http://www.ccuvs.com
The Canadian Centre for Unmanned Vehicle Systems is a nonprofit formed to
    facilitate sustained, profitable growth in the Canadian civil and commercial
    unmanned systems sector.

Drone Advocates for Public Safety
P.O. Box 2344
Decatur, GA 30031
Website: http://www.droneadvocates.org
Drone Advocates for Public Safety is dedicated to reducing injuries, deaths, and
    economic damage by ensuring public safety organizations access to the newest
    aerial safety technology.

Federal Aviation Administration (FAA)
US Department of Transportation
800 Independence Avenue, SW
Washington, DC 20591
(866) TELL-FAA
Website: http://www.faa.gov
The Federal Aviation Administration (FAA) is the US government agency in charge
    of ensuring the safety of all civil, including commercial, aviation.

Professional Aerial Photographers Association
12069 Cessna Place
Brookshire, TX 77423
(800) 373-2135
Website: http://professionalaerialphotographers.com
The Professional Aerial Photographers' Association is a professional trade organiza-
    tion for aerial photographers around the world.

Unmanned Aerial Vehicle Systems Association (UAVSA)
Los Angeles, California
(866) 691-7776
Website: http://www.uavsa.org/about
Founded in 2014, the Unmanned Aerial Vehicle Systems Association (UAVSA) is the leading association serving the growing UAS/drone community.

# LIST OF WEBSITES

Because of the changing nature of internet links, Rosen Publishing has developed an online list of websites related to the subject of this book. This site is updated regularly. Please use this link to access the list:

http://www.rosenlinks.com/IWD/photo

# FOR FURTHER READING

Babler, Jason. *Make: Volume 44: Fun with Drones!* San Francisco, CA: Maker Media, 2015.

Baichtal, John. *Building Your Own Drones: A Beginners Guide.* Indianapolis, IN: Que Publishing, 2015.

Dougherty, Martin. *Drones: An Illustrated Guide to the Unmanned Aircraft That Are Filling Our Skies.* London, England: Amber Books, 2015.

*Drones.* Farmington Hills, MI: Greenhaven Press, 2016.

Gerdes, Louise I. *Drones* (At Issue). Farmington Hills, MI: Greenhaven Press, 2014.

Kallen, Stuart. *What Is the Future of Drones?* San Diego, CA: Referencepoint Press, 2016.

Kilby, Terry, and Belinda Kilby. *Getting Started with Drones: Build and Customize Your Own Quadcopter.* San Francisco, CA: Maker Media, 2015.

Marsico, Katie. *Drones.* New York, NY: Scholastic Library Publishing, 2016.

Norris, Donald. *Build Your Own Quadcopter.* New York, NY: McGraw-Hill Education, 2014.

Rauf, Don. *Getting the Most Out of Makerspaces to Build Unmanned Aerial Vehicles.* New York, NY: Rosen Publishing Group, 2014.

Ripley, Tim. *Military Jobs: Drone Operators.* New York, NY: Cavendish Square Publishing, 2015.

Wesselhoeft, Conrad. *Dirt Bikes, Drones and Other Ways to Fly.* New York, NY: Houghton Mifflin Harcourt, 2015.

# BIBLIOGRAPHY

"Benefits of Drones." Beeaerial.co.uk. Retrieved May 17, 2016. http://www.beeaerial .co.uk/benefits-using-drones-aerial-filming-uk.

Betters, Elyse. "Drone Aerial Photography Explained: Here's What it Is and How To Do It." Pocket-lint, August 7, 2014. http://www.pocket-lint.com /news/130253-drone-aerial-photography-explained-here-s-what-it-is-and -how-to-do-it.

"Capture a Bird's-Eye View With an Aerial Photography Career." The Art Career Project. Retrieved May 16, 2016. http://www.theartcareerproject.com/aeri- al-photography/902.

Cornforth, John. "How-To: Using a Drone for Dramatic Nature Photos." *Popular Photography*, February 19, 2015. http://www.popphoto.com/how-to/2015/02/ how-to-using-drone-dramatic-nature-photos.

DuMonthier, Asha. "The Next Wave in Photography – Drones." New America Media, August 13, 2013. http://newamericamedia.org/2013/08/the-next-wave -in-photography----aerial-drones.php.

Evans, Carter. "Paparazzi Now Using Drones to Hunt Down and Photograph Stars." CBS News, August 23, 2014. http://www.cbsnews.com/news/paparazzi-take-to- the-skies-to-pursue-stars-with-drones.

Federal Aviation Administration. "FAA Announces Exemptions for Commercial UAS Movie and TV Production." Dronelife.com, September 24, 2015. http:// dronelife.com/2014/09/25/faa-announces-exemptions-commercial-uas-mov- ie-tv-production.

Goglia, John. "FAA Says Media Can Use Drone Photos From Citizen Journalists, Not Professionals." *Forbes*, May 7, 2015. http://www.forbes.com/sites /johngoglia/2015/05/07/faa-says-media-can-use-drone-photos-from-citizen -journalists-not-professionals/#632be3f61ebc.

Lavigne, Paula. "Eyes in the Sports Sky." ESPN, May 29, 2014. http://espn.go.com/ espn/otl/story/_/id/10974559/drones-use-ucla-mlb-starting-show-more-sports -fields-coaches-embrace-technology.

Mazza, Ed "Cirque du Soleil's Drone Video, 'Sparked,' Is Pure Magic." *Huffington Post*, September 23, 2014. http://www.huffingtonpost.com/2014/09/22/cirque -du-soleil-sparked-drone-video_n_5865668.html.

McNicholas, Robin. "Will 2016 be the Year When Drones Become Art?" *Guardian*, December 19, 2014. https://www.theguardian.com/culture-professionals-ne twork/2014/dec/19/2015-drones-art-creative-examples.

Megerian, Chris. "Gov. Jerry Brown Approves New Limits on Paparazzi Drones." *Los Angeles Times*, October 6, 2015. http://www.latimes.com/local/political/la-pol-sac-brown-drones-paparazzi-20151006-story.html.

Mullin, Benjamin. "Why 2016 Could Be a Breakout Year for Drone Journalism." Poynter.com, January 11, 2016. http://www.poynter.org/2016/why-2016-could-be-a-breakout-year-for-drone-journalism/390386.

Murphy, Mike. "Drone Racing Just Became a Mainstream Sport, Thanks to ESPN." *Quartz*, April 13, 2016. http://qz.com/660282/drone-racing-just-became-a-mainstream-sport-thanks-to-espn.

Nofuente, Kyle. "Hivemapper, The Google Maps For Drones, Launches Beta App on Play Store." *Tech Times*, November 5, 2015. http://www.techtimes.com/articles/103674/20151105/hivemapper-the-google-maps-for-drones-launches-beta-app-on-play-store.htm#sthash.3v6CdbUD.dpuf.

Popper, Ben. "The FAA Just Took a Huge Step Towards Legalizing Commercial Drone Flights." *The Verge*, February 15, 2015. http://www.theverge.com/2015/2/15/8040647/faa-small-uav-drone-rules-regulations.

Samuels, Liron. "Gorgeous Aerial Drone Photos that would be Totally Illegal Today." *DIY Photography*, April 9, 2015. http://www.diyphotography.net/gorgeous-aerial-drone-photos-that-would-be-totally-illegal-today.

Toor, Amar. "National Geographic Uses Drones and Robots to Capture Stunning Images of African Lions." *The Verge*, August 9, 2013. http://www.theverge.com/2013/8/9/4604876/national-geographic-living-with-lions-serengeti-robot-drone-photography.

Ungerleider, Neal. "How Drones Are Transforming The Way You Shop For Real Estate." *Fast Company*, February 27, 2016. http://www.fastcompany.com/3056615/how-drones-are-transforming-the-real-estate-industry.

"Use of Drones in Sports Broadcasts." Stats.com. December 16, 2015. http://www.stats.com/blog/2015/12/16/use-of-drones-in-sports-broadcasts.

Verrier, Richard. "Drones are Providing Film and TV Viewers a New Perspective on the Action." *Los Angeles Times*, October 8, 2015. http://www.latimes.com/entertainment/envelope/cotown/la-et-ct-drones-hollywood-20151008-story.html.

# INDEX

## W

## Y

# ABOUT THE AUTHOR

Laura La Bella is the author of more than forty nonfiction children's books. She has profiled actress and activist Angelina Jolie in *Celebrity Activists: Angelina Jolie Goodwill Ambassador to the UN*; reported on the declining availability of the world's fresh water supply in *Not Enough to Drink: Pollution, Drought, and Tainted Water Supplies*; and has examined the food industry in *Safety and the Food Supply*. La Bella lives in Rochester, New York, with her husband and two sons.

# PHOTO CREDITS